My Healthy Lean and Green Cooking Guide

Super Simple Recipes to Stay Fit & Healthy

Roxana Sutton

TABLE OF CONTENTS

Roast Chicken Stuffed Avocados

Prep Time: 5 mins

Cook Time: 10 mins

Ingredients

- 1 avocados pitted
- 2 cups roast chicken shredded
- 1/3 cup tomato seeded and diced
- 1/4 cup shredded cheese Mexican blend
- 1/4 cup cilantro stems chopped
- 2 Tablespoon mayonnaise
- 1 Tablespoon Sriracha optional
- Mozzarella cheese to top

Instructions

Preheat the air fryer at 400F (200C) for 2 minutes.

Mix all the ingredients, except Mozzarella cheese, and them on top of avocados. Place them inside the fryer basket.

Sprinkle some mozzarella cheese over the chicken mixture and let the cheese melt for 1 minute in the preheated air fryer.

Air fry at 360F (180C) for 4-5 minutes until the cheese is slightly golden brown.

Nutrition

Calories:349kcal | Carbohydrates: 9g | Protein: 21g | Fat: 26g | Saturated Fat: 5g | Cholesterol: 61mg | Sodium: 235mg | Potassium: 677mg | Fiber: 7g | Sugar: 1g | Vitamin C: 14mg | Calcium: 56mg | Iron: 1mg

Kimchi Chicken

Prep Time: 35 mins

Cook Time: 15 mins

Ingredients

- 1/2 pound of chicken thigh cut into thin slices
- 1/3 cup kimchi juice from kimchi jar
- 2 Tablespoon of grated ginger
- 1 teaspoon soy sauce
- 1/2 teaspoon corn starch
- 1/4 cup kimchi sliced or to taste
- 1 green onion thinly sliced

Instructions

Mix the chicken slices with corn starch, kimchi sauce, grated ginger, and soy sauce. Marinate for at least 30 minutes.

In a lightly greased cake pan, air fry the chicken at 380F (190C) for about 10-12 minutes until the meat is cooked through. When done, add in chopped kimchi and stir. Air fry at 380F (190C) for 2 more minutes.

Garnish with green onion to serve.

Nutrition

Calories: 146kcal | Carbohydrates: 2g | Protein: 22g | Fat: 5g | Saturated Fat: 1g | Cholesterol: 108mg | Sodium: 270mg | Potassium: 307mg | Fiber: 1g | Sugar: 1g | Vitamin C: 1mg | Calcium: 10mg | Iron: 1mg

Garlic Parmesan Chicken Tenderloins

Prep Time: 10 mins

Cook Time: 15 mins

Ingredients

- 4-6 pieces of chicken tenderloins defrosted and pat dry
- 1 egg beaten
- 1 Tablespoon Italian seasoning
- 1/2 cup shredded Parmesan cheese
- 1 teaspoon garlic powder
- 1/2 teaspoon paprika
- 1/4 teaspoon cayenne pepper or to taste

Instructions

In a shallow plate, mix all the dry ingredients and set aside.

Dip the tenderloins into egg then dredge them in seasoning mix.

Place the tenderloins in the fryer basket and air fry at 380F (190C) for 10-12 minutes, flip once in the middle, until the chicken is cooked through at 165F (74C) and the surface is golden brown.

Nutrition

Calories: 384kcal | Carbohydrates: 58g | Protein: 16g | Fat: 12g | Saturated Fat: 2g | Sodium: 44mg | Potassium: 737mg | Fiber: 15g | Sugar: 12g | | Vitamin C: 45mg | Calcium: 127mg | Iron: 6mg

Easy Chicken With Creamed Spinach

Prep Time: 5 mins

Cook Time: 15 mins

Ingredients For Chicken:

- 4 boneless skinless chicken (thighs, breasts, or tenderloins)
- 1 tablespoon olive oil
- 1/2 teaspoon paprika
- 1/2 teaspoon garlic powder
- 1/2 teaspoon onion powder
- 1/2 teaspoon dried basil
- Salt and pepper to taste

Ingredients For Creamed Spinach:

- 2 cans of Campbell Cream of Chicken Soup
- 1 can of water using the soup cans
- 1 Tablespoon olive oil
- 1/2 yellow onion diced
- 4 garlic cloves minced
- 8 ounces baby spinach or chopped spinach

- 1/3 cup grated Parmesan cheese or to taste

Instructions

In a small bowl, mix all the dry ingredients for the chicken and set aside.

Use a paper towel to pat dry the chicken pieces and rub them with olive oil. Season both sides of the chicken with the seasoning mixture and place them inside the fryer basket. Air fry at 380F (190C) for 10-12 minutes, flip once in the middle until the chicken is fully cooked and the internal meat temperature exceeds 165F (74C).

In the meantime, use a skillet to saute the onion and garlic in olive oil until the onion is translucent. Stir in two cans of soup and one can of water and bring it to boil. Then, turn the heat to low and stir in the cheese.

When the chicken is done, transfer the chicken to the skillet and add in the spinach. Let it simmer for 2- 3 minutes until the spinach wilts.

Nutrition

Calories: 250kcal | Carbohydrates: 5g | Protein: 29g | Fat: 12g | Saturated Fat: 3g | Cholesterol: 78mg | Sodium: 313mg | Potassium: 767mg | Fiber: 2g | Sugar: 1g | Vitamin C: 19mg | Calcium: 172mg | Iron: 2mg

Easy Dry Rub Chicken

Prep Time: 5 mins

Cook Time: 15 mins

Ingredients

- 4 skin-on boneless chicken thighs
- 2 Tablespoon olive oil
- 1 Tablespoon Italian seasoning
- 2 teaspoons paprika
- 2 teaspoons garlic powder
- 2 teaspoons onion powder
- 1/2 teaspoon salt
- 1/2 teaspoon black pepper

Instructions

Mix all the dry ingredients and set aside.

Make a few slices on the flesh part of the chicken thigh without cutting through. Use a paper towel to pat dry the thighs.

Rub both sides of the chicken with olive oil. Then, rub both sides of the chicken generously with the dry mix.

Line the fryer basket with lightly greased aluminum foil. Put the chicken thighs into the basket without stacking. Air fry at 360F (180C) for about 8 minutes. Then, air fry again at 400F (200C) for about 4 minutes until cooked through at 165F (74C).

Nutrition

Calories: 324kcal | Carbohydrates: 4g | Protein: 19g | Fat: 26g | Saturated Fat: 6g | Cholesterol: 111mg | Sodium: 381mg | Potassium: 298mg | Fiber: 1g | Sugar: 1g | Vitamin A: 602IU | Vitamin C: 1mg | Calcium: 33mg | Iron: 2mg

Breaded Parmesan Chicken

Prep Time: 10 mins

Cook Time: 15 mins

Ingredients

- 4 boneless skinless chicken thighs
- 1 egg
- 2 Tablespoon milk
- Salt and pepper to taste
- 3/4 cups Italian breadcrumbs. If using regular breadcrumbs, add 2 teaspoons of Italian seasoning to the bread crumbs.
- 1/3 cup freshly grated Parmesan cheese
- 1 1/2 teaspoon garlic powder
- Olive oil in a spritzer

Instructions

Mix egg and milk in a shallow dish and season with salt and pepper.

In a shallow dish, mix bread crumbs, Parmesan cheese, and garlic powder.

Dab dry the chicken thighs with paper towels. Dip chicken thighs in the egg mixture and dredge both sides with bread crumbs mix.

Place thighs inside the fryer basket without stacking and spray some olive oil on chicken thighs.

Air fry at 380F (190C) for 10-12 minutes until the thighs are fully cooked through when the internal temperature exceeds 165F (74C).

Nutrition

Calories: 281kcal | Carbohydrates: 17g | Protein: 30g | Fat: 10g | Saturated Fat: 3g | Cholesterol: 157mg

| Sodium: 548mg | Potassium: 378mg | Fiber: 1g | Sugar: 2g | Vitamin A: 202IU | Vitamin C: 1mg | Calcium: 158mg | Iron: 2mg

Fusion Chicken Wrap

Prep Time: 5 mins

Cook Time: 15 mins

Ingredients For Chicken:

- 3 pieces of skinless boneless chicken thighs or breast, thinly sliced
- 3 Tablespoon soy sauce
- 1 Tablespoon garlic powder
- 1 teaspoon corn starch
- 1 teaspoon Chinese five spices powder
- 1/4 teaspoon black pepper

Other Ingredients:

- 4 Tortillas
- 1/3 cup Hoisin sauce or to taste
- 1/2 cup thinly sliced green onion
- Green salad optional

Instructions

Mix all the ingredients for the chicken and marinate for at least one hour in the refrigerator. Air fry at 380F (190C) for 10-12 minutes, stir 1-2 times in between until chicken is fully cooked through.

To assemble, spread some Hoisin sauce onto a piece of tortilla. Put some green onion, chicken, and come green salad (optional) on the tortilla and wrap it up.

Nutrition

Calories: 163kcal | Carbohydrates: 29g | Protein: 5g | Fat: 3g | Saturated Fat: 1g | Cholesterol: 1mg | Sodium: 454mg | Potassium: 160mg | Fiber: 2g | Sugar: 8g | Vitamin A: 125IU | Vitamin C: 2mg | Calcium: 51mg | Iron: 2mg

Honey Ginger Chicken

Prep Time: 3 hrs

Cook Time: 15 mins

Ingredients For Chicken:

- 4 pieces skin-on boneless chicken thighs
- 2 Tablespoon minced garlic
- 2 Tablespoons soy sauce
- 2 Tablespoons rice wine
- 2 Tablespoons honey
- 2 Tablespoon grated ginger

Instructions

In a Ziploc bag, combine all the ingredients for the chicken and marinate in the refrigerator for at least 3 hours or overnight. Remove from the refrigerator 30 minutes before air frying.

Line the fryer basket with a sheet of lightly greased aluminum foil. Put the chicken thighs in the basket skin side down without stacking. Air fry at 380F (190C) for about 7 minutes.

Turn the chicken thighs over so they are skin side up. Air fry again at 380F (190C) for 5-6 minutes until the chicken is cooked through when the internal temperature exceeds 165F (74C). Save the juices on the foil to drizzle over rice if desired.

Sprinkle some green onion and sesame seeds to serve.

Nutrition

Calories: 63kcal | Carbohydrates: 12g | Protein: 2g | Fat: 1g | Saturated Fat: 1g | Cholesterol: 1mg | Sodium: 506mg | Potassium: 67mg | Fiber: 1g | Sugar: 9g | Vitamin A: 62IU | Vitamin C: 2mg | Calcium: 17mg | Iron: 1mg

Three Cup Chicken

Prep Time: 40 mins

Cook Time: 20 mins

Ingredients For The Chicken:

- 1 pound boneless skinless thighs (about 500g) cut into one inch pieces
- 2 Tablespoon sesame oil
- 4 Tablespoon soy paste
- 3 Tablespoon rice wine
- 2 Tablespoon mirin
- 2 Tablespoon grated ginger

Other Ingredients:

- 2 teaspoon olive oil
- 5 cloves of garlic
- 6-7 slices of ginger
- Red chili pepper optional
- 1 teaspoon sesame oil
- 1 bunch of basil
- 2 green onion cut into one-inch pieces

Instructions

Mix all of the seasonings in the chicken ingredients and marinate the chicken with half of the marinade for about 30 minutes

Put the garlic cloves and ginger slices into the cake pan and drizzle them with 2 teaspoons of olive oil.

Air fry at 400F (200C) for about 2-3 minutes.

Add in the chicken along with its marinade and air fry at 380F (190C) for 10 minutes, stir two times in between. Add the rest of the marinade, 3/4 of the green onion, 3/4 of the basil, and chili pepper (optional), and stir. Air fry at 380F (190C) for 6-7 minutes stirring once in between until the chicken is cooked through.

When done, mix the rest of the basil and green onion and drizzle 1 teaspoon of sesame oil to serve.

Nutrition

Calories: 291kcal | Carbohydrates: 12g | Protein: 24g | Fat: 15g | Saturated Fat: 3g | Cholesterol: 108mg

| Sodium: 553mg | Potassium: 324mg | Fiber: 1g | Sugar: 5g | Vitamin A: 87IU | Vitamin C: 3mg | Calcium: 21mg | Iron: 1mg

Mushroom Chicken

Prep Time: 35 mins

Cook Time: 15 mins

Ingredients For Chicken:

- 1 tablespoon soy sauce
- 1 tablespoon Shaoxing wine
- 1 tablespoon corn starch

Ingredients for the sauce:

- 3 tablespoons oyster sauce
- 1 tablespoon Shaoxing wine
- 1 Tablespoon soy sauce
- 2 Tablespoon chicken stock
- 2 teaspoon grated ginger
- 1 teaspoon sugar
- 1/4 teaspoon black pepper

Other Ingredients:

- 1/4 lbs button mushroom
- 3 cloves garlic chopped
- 1 green onion cut into 1-inch pieces

- 1 teaspoon sesame oil

Instructions

Marinate the chicken with soy sauce, Shaoxing wine, and corn starch for at least 30 minutes. In a small bowl, mix all the ingredients for the sauce,

In a lightly greased cake, pan put garlic on the bottom of the pan then put in the marinated chicken. Air fry at 380F (190C) for 10 minutes stirring once in the middle.

Stir in the sauce and air and mushroom and air fry at 380F (190C) for about 4 minutes until the chicken is cooked through.

When done, stir in the sesame oil and green onion to serve.

Nutrition

Calories: 57kcal | Carbohydrates: 8g | Protein: 2g | Fat: 1g | Saturated Fat: 1g | Cholesterol: 1mg | Sodium: 885mg | Potassium: 118mg | Fiber: 1g | Sugar: 2g | Vitamin C: 2mg | Calcium: 8mg | Iron: 1mg

Thai Basil Chicken

Prep Time: 45 mins

Cook Time: 15 mins

Ingredients For Chicken:

- 1/2 pound boneless skinless chicken thighs thinly sliced
- 3 tablespoons minced garlic
- 1 tablespoons fish sauce
- 1/2 tablespoons olive oil
- 1 teaspoon sugar or to taste
- 1 teaspoon corn starch
- 1/2 Tablespoon dark soy sauce
- 1/2 teaspoon light soy sauce
- 1/2 tablespoon oyster sauce
- 1/4 teaspoon white pepper powder

Instructions

Marinate the chicken in all the meat ingredients for about 30 minutes.

In a lightly greased cake pan, air fry the onion at 320F (160C) for about 3-4 minutes. Put the marinated chicken over the onion and air fry at 380F (190C) for about 10 minutes until the meat is cooked through, stirring twice in between.

Finally, stir in the basil leaves, jalapeno, and chicken broth into the cake pan. Air fry again at 380F (190C) for 2 minutes.

Serve over rice or when done.

Nutrition

Calories:132kcal | Carbohydrates: 10g | Protein: 13g | Fat: 4g | Saturated Fat: 1g | Cholesterol: 54mg | Sodium: 572mg | Potassium: 259mg | Fiber: 1g | Sugar: 5g | Vitamin C: 5mg | Calcium: 30mg | Iron: 1mg

Salt And Pepper Wings

Prep Time: 30 mins

Cook Time: 25 mins

Ingredients For The Wings:

- 18 chicken wings
- 3 Tablespoon soy sauce
- 1 Tablespoon minced garlic
- 2 teaspoon sugar
- 2 teaspoon rice wine
- 1 teaspoon sesame oil
- 2 egg yolks

Other ingredients:

- 1/2 cup tapioca starch
- Thinly sliced red chili pepper or jalapeno optional
- 2 tablespoon thinly sliced green onion
- Salt to taste
- White pepper powder to taste
- Chopped cilantro for garnish

Instructions

In a Ziploc bag, marinate the wings with all the other wing ingredients combined for at least 30 minutes in the refrigerator.

Add the tapioca starch into the bag and shake. Let the bag sit at room temperature. When you see the tapioca starch appears to be moist (no longer white), put them in the fryer basket. Air fry at 380F (190C) for 20-22 minutes, turn the wings twice in between. During the second turn, put in the hot chili peppers and continue to air fry until the wings exceed 165F (74C) and the skin is crispy.

Place the wings in a large mixing bowl and toss with the salt, pepper, green onion, and cilantro. Serve the wings while still hot.

Nutrition

Calories: 394kcal | Carbohydrates: 11g | Protein: 28g | Fat: 25g | Saturated Fat: 7g | Cholesterol: 176mg

| Sodium: 611mg | Potassium: 251mg | Fiber: 1g | Sugar: 2g | Vitamin C: 2mg | Calcium: 29mg | Iron: 2mg

Roasted Cornish Hen

Prep Time: 5 mins

Cook Time: 40 mins

Ingredients

- 1 Cornish hen completely defrosted and pat dry
- 1/2 teaspoon salt
- 1/2 teaspoon Italian seasoning
- 1/2 teaspoon paprika
- 1/2 teaspoon garlic powder
- 1/4 teaspoon black pepper

Instructions

Combine all the dried ingredients and set them aside. Put a steamer rack inside an aluminum lined fryer basket.

Generously rub the surface of the Cornish hen with seasoning mix and place the Cornish hen on the rack with the breast side facing up. Spray some oil on the Cornish hen. Stick the thermometer probe inside the breast and covered the hen with a sheet of aluminum foil. If possible, use another steamer rack to hold the foil down.

Air fry at 390F (195C) for about 30 minutes. Remove the foil and air fry again at 390F (195C) for another 7-8 minutes until the temperature of the breast exceeds 170F (77C).

Leave the Cornish hen in the air fryer for 10 minutes before serving.

Nutrition

Calories:228kcal | Carbohydrates: 1g | Protein: 19g | Fat: 16g | Saturated Fat: 4g | Cholesterol: 114mg | Sodium: 360mg | Potassium: 266mg | Fiber: 1g | Sugar: 1g | Vitamin C: 1mg | Calcium: 16mg | Iron: 1mg

Miso Marinated Chicken

Prep Time: 3 hrs

Total Time: 20 mins

Ingredients

- 3 boneless chicken thighs
- 3 Tablespoon miso
- 1 Tablespoon soy sauce
- 1 Tablespoon mirin
- 1 Tablespoon rice wine

Instructions

Combine miso, soy sauce, mirin, and rice wine and mix well. Marinate the chicken with the sauce mixture in the refrigerator for at least 3 hours or overnight.

Take the chicken out of the refrigerator 30 minute before air frying.

Place the chicken thighs skin-side down in the fryer basket lined with lightly greased aluminum foil. Air fry at 380F (190C) for about 12 minutes. Flip, then air fry again at 380F (190C) for 6-7 minutes or until the meat temperature exceeds 165 (74C).

Nutrition

Calories:225kcal | Carbohydrates: 6g | Protein: 16g | Fat: 15g | Saturated Fat: 4g | Cholesterol: 83mg | Sodium: 825mg | Potassium: 210mg | Fiber: 1g | Sugar: 2g | Vitamin A: 66IU | Calcium: 14mg | Iron: 1mg

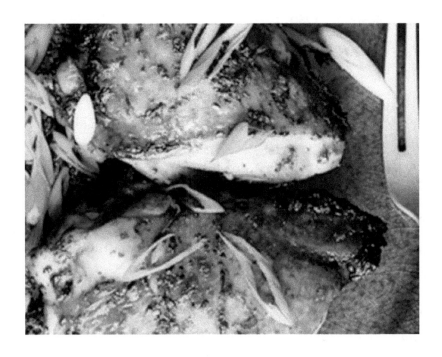

Black Bean Sauce Marinated Chicken

Prep Time: 4 mins

Cook Time: 20 mins

Ingredients

- 3 boneless chicken thighs
- 1 Tablespoon Black Bean Sauce
- 1 Tablespoon oyster sauce
- 1 Tablespoon mirin
- 1 Tablespoon rice wine
- Thinly sliced green onion to garnish

Instructions

Combine the black bean sauce, oyster sauce, mirin, and rice wine. Marinate the chicken with the sauce mixture and refrigerate for at least 3 hours or overnight.

Take the chicken out of the refrigerator 30 minute before air frying. Line the fryer basket with lightly greased aluminum foil.

Place the chicken thighs in the fryer basket skin side down and air fry at 380F (190C) for about 12 minutes. Flip, then air fry again at 380F (190C) for 6-7 minutes or until the meat temperature exceeds 165 (74C). Save the drippings.

Thinly slice the chicken, garnish with green onion, and drizzle with some drippings to serve.

Nutrition

Calories: 204kcal | Carbohydrates: 3g | Protein: 14g | Fat: 14g | Saturated Fat: 4g | Cholesterol: 83mg | Sodium: 357mg | Potassium: 174mg | Fiber: 1g | Sugar: 1g | Calcium: 7mg | Iron: 1mg

Tomato And Pesto Chicken

Prep Time: 5 mins

Cook Time: 20 mins

Ingredients

- 2 skinless and boneless chicken thighs
- 1-2 Roma tomatoes cut into 1/4 inch slices
- 1/4 cup pesto sauce
- 1/3 cup shredded Mozzarella cheese
- black pepper to taste
- 1/2 teaspoon parsley flakes

Instructions

Cover the chicken thighs with a large piece of saran wrap. Use a heavy object or a rolling pin to lightly pound the chicken so the thighs are somewhat flattened and even in thickness throughout.

Line the fryer basket with a sheet of lightly greased aluminum foil. Place the thighs in the basket and sprinkle with some black pepper.

Scoop and spread about 2 tablespoons of pesto sauce onto the chicken thighs and top them with a layer of tomato slices. Air fry at 360F (180C) for 14 minutes.

Sprinkle Mozzarella cheese over the tomato slices and air fry at 380F (190C) for about 4-5 minutes until meat temperature exceeds 165F (74C).

Garnish with some parsley to serve.

Nutrition

Calories: 429kcal | Carbohydrates: 4g | Protein: 24g | Fat: 34g | Saturated Fat: 10g | Cholesterol: 128mg

| Sodium: 496mg | Potassium: 305mg | Fiber: 1g | Sugar: 2g | Vitamin C: 4mg | Calcium: 153mg | Iron: 1mg

Chicken Fajitas

Prep Time: 45 mins

Cook Time: 20 mins

Ingredients For The Chicken:

- 1 1/2 pound skinless boneless chicken thighs (about 750g) cut into strips ù1/2 cup chopped onion
- 1 Tablespoon olive oil
- 1 lime juiced
- 1 teaspoon salt
- 1 1/2 teaspoon ground cumin
- 1 1/2 teaspoon garlic powder
- 1 teaspoon chili powder
- 1/2 teaspoon paprika

Instructions

Combine all the ingredients for the chicken and marinate it in the refrigerator for at least 30 minutes. Cut the bell peppers into thin slices and microwave for about 2-3 minutes.

Air fry chicken strips on a lightly greased aluminum foil or a baking pan at 320F (160C) for about 16- 18 minutes until all the meat is cooked through, stirring every 3-4 minutes. During the last stir, mix in the bell pepper and continue to air fry until completion.

To serve, wrap the chicken with tortilla and top it with chopped green onion, cilantro, cheese, and sour cream if desired.

Nutrition

Calories: 265kcal | Carbohydrates: 7g | Protein: 34g | Fat: 11g | Saturated Fat: 2g | Cholesterol: 162mg | Sodium: 747mg | Potassium: 574mg | Fiber: 2g | Sugar: 2g | Vitamin C: 39mg | Calcium: 37mg | Iron: 2mg

Keto Muffins

Prep Time: 5 mins

Cook Time: 15 mins

Ingredients

- 8 oz ground turkey or chicken
- 1 teaspoon garlic powder
- 1/4 cup shredded cheese
- 1/4 teaspoon black pepper
- 1 egg beaten
- 1/4 cup chopped basil
- 1/4 cup chopped green onion
- 2 Tablespoon chopped pickled jalapeno optional
- 1/4 teaspoon salt

Instructions

In a large bowl, mix the ground turkey, garlic powder, shredded cheese, and black pepper. Divide the ground meat mixture into four portions.

Lightly grease the muffin cups. Scoop one portion of the ground meat into each cup then press it against the walls and form it into a cup shape. Air fry at 380F (190C) for 6 minutes.

In the meantime, mix the egg with basil, green onion, and salt. Then, scoop the egg mixture into each cup and air fry again at 380F (190C) for another 6-7 minutes until the egg is cook through.

Nutrition

Calories: 107kcal | Carbohydrates: 2g | Protein: 17g | Fat: 4g | Saturated Fat: 2g | Cholesterol: 78mg | Sodium: 319mg | Potassium: 218mg | Fiber: 1g | Sugar: 1g | Vitamin C: 2mg | Calcium: 49mg | Iron: 1mg

Basil Chicken Zucchini Wrap

Prep Time: 10 mins

Cook Time: 15 mins

Ingredients

- 1 large chicken breast butterflied
- 1 medium zucchini cut into 1/4 inch thick slices
- 7-8 basil leaves
- 1/4 teaspoon black pepper
- 4 strips of bacon

Instructions

On a cutting board, cover the butterflied chicken breast with a large sheet of saran wrap. Use a rolling pin or a heavy object to pound the chicken so the thickness is even throughout. Then, cut the chicken into 4 pieces.

Sprinkle some black pepper onto the chicken. Then, put the zucchini slice and 1 or 2 basil leaves on top of each chicken and roll it up. Finally, take one strip of bacon and wrap it around the chicken roll. Secure it with toothpicks if necessary.

Place a metal steamer rack inside the fryer basket and place the wraps on the rack. Air fry at 400F (200C) for 10-12 minutes or until the internal meat temp exceeds 165F (74C).

Nutrition

Calories:165kcal | Carbohydrates: 2g | Protein: 15g | Fat: 10g | Saturated Fat: 3g | Cholesterol: 51mg | Sodium: 215mg | Potassium: 381mg | Fiber: 1g | Sugar: 1g | Vitamin C: 9mg | Calcium: 11mg | Iron: 1mg

Garlic Chicken Roll

Prep Time: 45 mins

Cook Time: 20 mins

Ingredients

- 4 pieces of chicken breast or thigh
- 1/4 cup of minced garlic divided
- 4 teaspoon of rice wine divided
- 1 teaspoon of pink Himalayan salt divided
- white pepper powder to taste
- 2 Tablespoons of chopped fresh Thai basil optional

Instructions

Butterfly the chicken breast to make the breast into one large thinner piece and cover it with saran wrap. Use a rolling pin or a heavy pan to pound the meat so the chicken is uniform in thickness. Sprinkle 1 teaspoon rice wine, 1/4 teaspoon salt, 1 Tablespoon minced garlic, and some white pepper powder over each piece of chicken.

Roll the chicken up. Then, use a sheet of aluminum foil to wrap the chicken tightly the way one would wrap a candy (like Tootsie Roll). Refrigerate for at least 30 minutes.

Place the foil-wrapped chicken rolls in the fryer basket and air fry at 320F (160C) for 18-20 minutes. Check the internal meat temperature by inserting a food thermometer directly through the aluminum foil. The chicken is done when the temperature exceeds 165F (74C). Let cool before cutting it into slices.

This dish is usually served chilled. Sprinkle some chopped fresh Thai basil to serve.

Nutrition

Calories: 181kcal | Carbohydrates: 3g | Protein: 31g | Fat: 4g | Saturated Fat: 1g | Cholesterol: 91mg | Sodium: 747mg | Potassium: 559mg | Fiber: 1g | Sugar: 1g | Vitamin C: 4mg | Calcium: 22mg | Iron: 1mg

Cheesy Chicken Balls

Prep Time: 10 mins

Cook Time: 15 mins

Ingredients

- 10 oz Ground chicken or turkey 300g
- 1 egg
- 1/4 cup minced yellow onion
- 1/2 teaspoon garlic powder
- 1/2 teaspoon parsley flakes
- 1/4 teaspoon salt
- 1/4 teaspoon black pepper
- Cheddar cheese cubes or take the slices of cheese together
- 1/4 cup Japanese Panko about 14g carbs (Optional)
- 1/4 cup mayo
- 2 Tablespoon Sriracha hot sauce or to taste
- 1-2 Tablespoon honey optional

Instructions

Mix ground chicken, egg, onion, garlic powder, parsley flakes, salt, and black pepper together.

Take a cube of cheddar and wrap the ground meat around it. Roll it in the Panko and place it inside the parchment-lined fryer basket. Air fry at 360F (180C) for 12-14 minutes, turn the chicken cheese balls once in the middle until the meat is cooked through.

in the meantime, mix the mayo, Sriracha, and honey. To serve, drizzle the sriracha mayo over the chicken cheese balls or use it as a dip.

Nutrition

Calories: 273kcal | Carbohydrates: 9g | Protein: 22g | Fat: 17g | Saturated Fat: 5g | Cholesterol: 98mg | Sodium: 556mg | Potassium: 259mg | Fiber: 1g | Sugar: 5g | Vitamin C: 6mg | Calcium: 94mg | Iron: 1mg

Chicken Zucchini Boats

Prep Time: 30 mins

Cook Time: 15 mins

Ingredients

- 3 Medium Zucchini
- 8 oz ground or finely chopped chicken (about 250g)
- 1/4 cup finely chopped kimchi optional
- 1 Tablespoon oyster sauce
- 1 teaspoon Gochujang Korean hot pepper sauce
- 1 teaspoon sesame seeds
- 1 teaspoon sesame oil
- 1/2 teaspoon corn starch
- 1/3 cup Mozzarella cheese
- 2-3 tablespoon thinly sliced fresh basil

Instructions

Marinate the chicken with all the ingredients, except Mozzarella cheese and basil, for at least 30 minutes.

Line the fryer basket with a grill mat or a sheet of lightly greased aluminum foil. Cut zucchini lengthwise to about 1/4-1/2 inch thickness and put them side by side inside the fryer basket. Top the zucchini slices with ground meat mixture and air fry at 360F (180C) for about 8 minutes.

Sprinkle cheese over ground chicken and let it melt in the air fryer unit for about 1 minute. Then, air fry at 380F (190C) for about 3 minutes until the cheese is lightly golden brown.

Sprinkle with some thinly sliced fresh basil leaves to serve.

Nutrition

Calories: 183kcal | Carbohydrates: 4g | Protein: 14g | Fat: 12g | Saturated Fat: 4g | Cholesterol: 50mg | Sodium: 229mg | Potassium: 363mg | Fiber: 1g | Sugar: 3g | Vitamin C: 18mg | Calcium: 74mg | Iron: 1mg

Air Fryer Chicken Tenders

Prep Time: 5 Mins

Cook Time: 30 Mins

Total Time: 35 Mins

Yield: 4 Servings

Ingredients

- 12 chicken tenders, (1 1/4 lbs)
- 2 large eggs, beaten
- 1 teaspoon kosher salt
- Black pepper, to taste
- 1/2 cup seasoned breadcrumbs
- 1/2 cup seasoned panko
- Olive oil spray
- Lemon wedges, for serving

Instructions

Season chicken with salt and pepper.

Place egg in a shallow bowl. In a second shallow bowl, combine the bread crumbs and panko.

Dip chicken in the egg, then into the breadcrumb mixture and shake off excess, and place on a large dish or cutting board. Spray both sides of the chicken generously with oil.

Preheat air fryer to 400F.

In batches, cook the chicken 5 to 6 minutes on each side, until the chicken is cooked through and crispy and golden on the outside. Serve with lemon wedges.

Nutrient Value

Calories: 291kcal| Carbohydrates: 16.5g| Protein: 38.5g| Fat: 7g| Saturated Fat: 2g| Cholesterol: 197mg| Sodium: 653mg| Fiber: 1g| Sugar: 1.5g

Air Fryer Fried Chicken

Prep Time: 10 minutes

Cook Time: 25 minutes

Total Time: 35 minutes

Ingredients

- Marinade
- ½ whole chicken cut into separate pieces (breast, thigh, wing, and leg)
- ½ cup hot sauce
- ½ cup buttermilk Seasoning
- ¾ cup All-Purpose Flour
- 2 tsp seasoning salt
- 1 tsp garlic powder
- 1 tsp onion powder
- 1 tsp Italian seasoning
- ½ tsp cayenne pepper
- Oil for spraying
- Canola or Vegetable

Instructions

Place chicken pieces in buttermilk and hot sauce. Place in refrigerator and allow to marinate anytime from 1-24 hours.

Whisk together all-purpose flour, seasoning salt, garlic powder, onion powder, Italian seasoning, and cayenne pepper in a bowl. Set aside.

Place a parchment liner in the Air Fryer basket.

Remove a piece of chicken from the buttermilk mixture and place in the flour mixture, coating all sides of the chicken and shaking off any excess flour. Place the chicken pieces in the basket in a single layer. Close the Air Fryer basket and set the temperature to 390 degrees Fahrenheit and the timer to 25 minutes. Start the Air Fryer.

After 13 minutes, open the air fryer and spray any flour spots on the chicken. Flip the chicken and spray the other side with oil, ensuring all the flour spots are covered. Close the air fryer and cook for 12 more minutes.

Once the timer is up, open the Air Fryer and check chicken pieces with a quick read thermometer. Chicken is done when it reaches an internal temperature of 165 degrees at the thickest part of the chicken.

Nutrition

Calories:318kcal | Carbohydrates:21g | Protein21g | Fat: 15g | Saturated Fat: 4g | Cholesterol: 74mg | Sodium: 2055mg | Potassium: 297mg | Fiber: 1g | Sugar: 2g | Vitamin C: 23.9mg | Calcium: 56mg | Iron: 2.3mg

Crispy Air Fryer Chicken Breast

American Prep Time: 10 minutes

Cook Time: 10 minutes

Total Time: 20 minutes

Servings: 4

Ingredients

- 2 large boneless skinless chicken breasts sliced into cutlets
- 1 tablespoon oil olive oil, canola, or vegetable oil
- ½ cup (25g) dried bread crumbs
- ½ teaspoon paprika
- ¼ teaspoon dried chili powder
- ¼ teaspoon ground black pepper
- ¼ teaspoon garlic powder
- ¼ teaspoon onion powder
- ¼ teaspoon cayenne pepper
- ½ teaspoon salt

Instructions

Breaded Version:

Put the chicken breasts in a bowl and drizzle with oil. Make sure that they're well coated. In a shallow dish, mix the dried bread crumbs with the spices until well combined.

Coat each chicken breast in bread crumbs, and transfer to your air fryer basket.

Air fry in the air fryer at 390°F or 200°C for 10-12 minutes. After the first 7 minutes, open the air fryer and flip the chicken on the other side then continue cooking (cook for 3 minutes, depending on the size of the chicken breast used).

Unbreaded Version:

Drizzle oil over your boneless skinless chicken breasts, and season with your favorite seasonings.

Place the seasoned chicken breasts in the Air Fryer basket breast side down, and air fry for 12-15 minutes flipping halfway through using kitchen tongs.

When the cooking time is up, remove from the Air Fryer immediately so that the chicken does not dry out. Allow resting for 5 minutes before serving.

Nutrition

Calories: 163kcal | Carbohydrates: 1g | Protein: 24g | Fat: 7g | Saturated Fat: 1g | Cholesterol: 72mg | Sodium: 423mg | Potassium: 418mg | Fiber: 1g | Sugar: 1g | Vitamin A: 220IU | Vitamin C: 1.3mg | Calcium: 6mg | Iron: 0.5mg

Air Fryer Chicken & Broccoli

Prep Time: 10 mins

Cook Time: 15 mins

Total Time: 25 mins

Servings: 4 Servings

Ingredients

- 1 pound (454 g) boneless skinless chicken breast, cut into bite-sized pieces
- 1/4-1/2 pound (113-226 g) broccoli, cut into florets (1-2 cups)
- 1/2 medium (0.5 medium) onion, sliced thick
- 2 tablespoons (30 ml) olive oil or grapeseed oil
- 1/2 teaspoon (2.5 ml) garlic powder
- 1 tablespoon (15 ml) fresh minced ginger
- 1 tablespoon (15 ml) low sodium soy sauce, or to taste (use tamari for gluten free)
- 1 teaspoon (5 ml) sesame seed oil
- 2 teaspoons (10 ml) rice vinegar (use distilled white vinegar for gluten free)
- 2 teaspoons (10 ml) hot sauce (optional)
- Additional salt, to taste

- Additional black pepper, to taste
- Serve with lemon wedges

Instructions

In a large bowl, combine chicken breast, broccoli, and onion. Toss ingredients together.

Make The Marinade:

In a bowl, combine oil, garlic powder, ginger, soy sauce, sesame oil, rice vinegar, and hot sauce. Add the chicken, broccoli, and onions to the marinade. Stir thoroughly to combine the marinade with chicken, broccoli, and onions.

Air Fry: Add ingredients to the air fry basket. Air fry 380°F for 16-20 minutes, shaking and gently tossing halfway through cooking. Make sure to toss so that everything cooks evenly.

Check chicken to make sure it's cooked through. If not, cook for additional 3-5 minutes. Add additional salt and pepper, to taste. Squeeze fresh lemon juice on top and serve warm.

Nutrition

Calories: 191kcal | Carbohydrates: 4g | Protein: 25g | Fat: 7g | Saturated Fat: 1g | Cholesterol: 72mg | Sodium: 328mg | Potassium: 529mg | Sugar: 1g | Vitamin C: 29.1mg | Calcium: 22mg | Iron: 0.7mg

Air-fried General Tso's Chicken

Active Time: 20 Mins

Total Time: 35 Mins

Ingredients

- 1 large egg
- 1 pound boneless, skinless chicken thighs, patted dry and cut into1 to 1 1/4-inch chunk
- 1/3 cup plus 2 tsp. cornstarch, divided
- 1/4 teaspoon kosher salt
- 1/4 teaspoon ground white pepper
- 7 tablespoons lower-sodium chicken broth
- 2 tablespoons lower-sodium soy sauce
- 2 tablespoons ketchup
- 2 teaspoons sugar
- 2 teaspoons unseasoned rice vinegar
- 1 1/2 tablespoons canola oil
- 3 to 4 chiles de árbol, chopped and seeds discarded
- 1 tablespoon finely chopped fresh ginger
- 1 tablespoon finely chopped garlic
- 2 tablespoons thinly sliced green onion, divided
- 1 teaspoon toasted sesame oil

- 1/2 teaspoon toasted sesame seeds

Ingredients

Beat egg in a large bowl, add chicken, and coat well. In another bowl, combine 1/3 cup cornstarch with salt and pepper. Transfer chicken with a fork to cornstarch mixture, and stir with a spatula to coat every piece.

Transfer chicken to air-fryer oven racks (or fryer basket, in batches), leaving a little space between pieces. Preheat the air-fryer at 400°F for 3 minutes. Add the battered chicken; cook for 12 to 16 minutes, giving things a shake midway. Let dry for 3 to 5 minutes. If chicken is still damp on one side, cook for 1 to 2 minutes more.

Whisk together the remaining 2 teaspoons cornstarch with broth, soy sauce, ketchup, sugar, and rice vinegar. Heat canola oil and chiles in a large skillet over medium heat. When gently sizzling, add the ginger and garlic; cook until fragrant, about 30 seconds.

Re-whisk cornstarch mixture; stir into mixture in skillet. Increase heat to medium-high. When sauce begins to bubble, add chicken. Stir to coat; cook until sauce thickens and nicely clings to chicken, about 1 1/2 minutes. Turn off heat; stir in 1 tablespoon green onion and sesame oil. Transfer to a serving plate, and top with sesame seeds and remaining 1 tablespoon green onion.

Nutritional Information

Calories: 302| Fat: 13g | Sat fat: 3g | Unsatfat: 10g | Protein: 26g| Carbohydrate: 18g | Fiber: 0g | Sugars: 4g | Added sugars: 2g | Sodium: 611mg

Air Fryer Chicken Wings

Prep Time: 10 Mins

Cook Time: 30 Mins

Total Time: 40 Mins

Ingredients

- 2 pounds (907 g) chicken wings
- Kosher salt, or sea salt, to taste
- Black pepper, to taste
- Garlic powder, optional

Instructions

If needed, pat dries the chicken wings. Season with salt, pepper, and optional garlic powder.

For an oil-free version, place an even layer in the air fryer basket/tray. Follow the air fry instructions below.

Air Fry

Air Fry wings at 400°F/205°C for 30-35 minutes or until crispy and cooked through. You must flip the wings over after the first

20 minutes of cooking. Or you might need an extra flip to get the wings crispy to your personal preference.

If using a sauce, toss with a little sauce, then air fry for another 2-4 minutes. Or you can just toss or dip the wings in the sauce after they are finished cooking.

Nutrient Value

Calories: 271kcal |Protein: 22g | Fat: 19g | Saturated Fat: 5g |Cholesterol: 94mg| Sodium: 89mg | Potassium: 191mg | Vitamin A: 180IU | Vitamin C: 0.8mg | Calcium: 15mg | Iron:

1.2mg

Air Fryer Nashville Hot Chicken Tender

Prep Time: 10 mins

Cook Time: 30 mins

Total Time: 40 mins

Ingredients

- 1 lb chicken tenders
- ¾ cup milk
- 2 tbsp hot sauce
- ¾ cup panko bread crumbs
- 1 tsp paprika
- ½ tsp italian seasoning
- ½ tsp salt
- ½ garlic powder
- ½ onion powder
- ¼ tsp black pepper
- Salt and pepper to taste
- Oil for spraying canola, olive oil, or any oil with a high smoke point
- Hot paste

- ½ cup peanut oil
- 2 tbsp brown sugar
- 1 ½ tbsp cayenne pepper
- 1 tsp paprika
- 1 tsp dry mustard
- 1 tsp garlic powder
- ½ tsp salt

Instructions

Season tenders with a little salt and pepper. Set aside. Create a dredging station by whisking milk and hot sauce in one bowl. In a separate bowl, mix panko bread crumbs, paprika, Italian seasoning, salt, garlic powder, onion powder, and black pepper.

Preheat your air fryer to 375 degrees Fahrenheit.

Start by coating chicken tenders with milk mixture and drain off excess milk, then coat chicken in panko bread crumbs mixture, ensuring all of the chicken is coated.

Place chicken in greased air fryer basket or use a parchment sheet liner. Cook on 375 degrees for 14-16 minutes, flipping and spraying chicken halfway through cooking, until chicken is fully cooked and has reached a temperature of at least 165 degrees Fahrenheit.

Meanwhile, when there are about 5 minutes left on the chicken, create the hot paste. Add peanut oil, brown sugar, cayenne pepper, paprika, dry mustard, garlic powder, and salt to a medium-sized saucepan over medium heat and whisk to combine. Once your mixture starts to bubble and simmer, remove from heat.

Once chicken tenders are done, remove from air fryer and add them to a large bowl. Pour the hot paste over the chicken and toss to combine, making sure hot sauce covers all of the chicken. Serve and enjoy.

Nutrition

Calories:488kcal|Carbohydrates:19g | Protein: 28g | Fat: 34g | Saturated Fat: 7g | Cholesterol: 77mg | Sodium: 998mg | Potassium: 583mg | Fiber: 2g | Sugar: 9g | Vitamin C: 8mg | Calcium: 89mg | Iron: 1mg

Air Fryer Sesame Chicken

Prep Time: 10 Minutes

Cook Time: 25 Minutes

Total Time: 35 Minutes

Ingredients

Chicken

- 6 Boneless, Skinless Chicken Thighs
- 1/2 Cup Cornstarch
- Olive Oil Spray

Sauce

- 1/4 Cup Soy Sauce or Gluten-Free Soy Sauce
- 2 Tbsp Brown Sugar
- 2 Tbsp Orange Juice
- 5 Tsp Hoisin Sauce or Gluten-Free Sauce
- 1/2 Tsp Ground Ginger
- 1 Garlic Clove, Crushed
- 1 Tbsp Cold Water
- 1 Tbsp Cornstarch
- 2 Tsp Sesame Seeds

Instructions

Cut the chicken into cubed chunks, then toss in a bowl with Cornstarch or Potato Starch. Use enough to coat the chicken evenly.

Place in the Air Fryer and cook according to your Air Fryer Manual for chicken. (Note - I cooked ours on 390* for 24 minutes, 12 minutes on each side.)When the chicken is in the air fryer, add a nice even coat of olive oil cooking spray, once it's in the air fryer, it works best to mix it up halfway through cook time and add a coat of spray.

While the chicken is cooking, in a small saucepan, begin to make the sauce.

Add the soy sauce, brown sugar, orange juice, hoisin sauce, ground ginger, and garlic to the saucepan on medium-high heat. Whisk this up until well combined.

Once the sugar has fully dissolved and a low boil is reached, whisk in the water and cornstarch.

Mix in the sesame seeds. (The sauce should only take about 5 minutes or less to make on the stove and then an additional 5 minutes to thicken up.)

Remove the sauce from the heat and set aside for 5 minutes to thicken.

Once the chicken is done, remove it from the air fryer and place it in a bowl, and then coat it with the sauce.

Serve topped over rice and beans.

Nutrition Information

Calories: 335| Total Fat: 12g| Saturated Fat: 3g| Trans Fat: 0g| Unsaturated Fat: 9g| Cholesterol: 137mg| Sodium: 1100mg| Carbohydrates: 28g| Fiber: 1g| Sugar: 6g| Protein: 30g

Air Fryer Chicken Parmesan

Prep Time: 10 min

Cook Time: 20 min

Ready in 30 min

Ingredients

- Chicken
- 4 boneless skinless chicken breasts (4 oz./125 g each)
- ¼ tsp (2 ml) salt
- ½ cup (125 ml) all-purpose flour
- 2 eggs
- 2 tbsp (30 ml) milk
- 1½ oz. (45 g) fresh parmesan cheese (⅓ cup/75 ml grated)
- ⅔ cup (150 ml) panko breadcrumbs
- 1 tbsp (15 ml) italian seasoning mix
- 8 oz. (250 g) fresh mozzarella cheese Pasta
- 3 cups (750 ml) cherry tomatoes
- 1 pkg (9 oz./275 g) refrigerated cheese-filled tortellini
- 1 oz. (30 g) fresh parmesan cheese (¼ cup/60 ml grated)
- ½ cup (125 ml) fresh basil leaves, loosely packed
- 1 tbsp (15 ml) olive oil

- 1 tbsp (15 ml) balsamic vinegar
- ¼ tsp (1 ml) salt

Directions

Season the chicken with salt. Add the flour to one Coating Tray. Whisk the eggs and milk together in a second coating tray. Grate the Parmesan with the Microplane Adjustable Coarse Grater and combine with the panko and seasoning in the third coating tray.

Coat each chicken breast in flour first, then the eggs, then the panko mixture.

Divide the chicken onto two cooking trays of the Deluxe Air Fryer. Place the trays on the top and middle racks.

Cut the tomatoes in half with the Close & Cut; place them on the drip tray of the air fryer. Turn the wheel to select the setting; press the wheel to select AIR FRY. Turn the wheel to adjust the time to 18 minutes. Press the wheel to start. Switch the trays with the chicken halfway through cooking (you'll hear beeps as a reminder). Cook until the internal temperature reaches 165°F (74°C).

Slice the mozzarella with the Quick Slice. When the chicken is halfway through cooking, add the tortellini to the 3-qt. (3-L) Micro - Cooker Plus with enough water to cover the pasta. Microwave, covered, on HIGH, for 8 minutes.

Drain the pasta and transfer it to a medium mixing bowl. Grate the Parmesan cheese into the bowl with the Microplane® Adjustable Fine Grater. Grate the basil into the bowl with the Herb Mill. Add the remaining pasta ingredients and toss to combine.

When the timer is up, top each chicken breast with the mozzarella. Turn the wheel to select the AIR FRY setting; press the wheel to select. Turn the wheel to adjust the time to 2 minutes. Press the wheel to start.

Add the tomatoes to the pasta mixture and serve with the chicken.

Nutrients Value

Calories: 620| Total Fat: 21 g| Saturated Fat: 7 g| Cholesterol: 160 mg| Sodium: 930 mg| Carbohydrate: 60g| Fiber: 1g| Total Sugars: 5g| Protein: 47g

Air Fryer Chicken Breast

Prep Time: 5 mins

Cook Time: 20 mins

Resting Time: 5 mins

Total Time: 30 mins

Ingredients

- 1.5 tbsp cornstarch
- 1.5 tsp garlic powder
- 1 tsp smoked paprika
- 1.5 tsp dried oregano
- 4 chicken breasts boneless
- Oil

Instructions

Prepare the chicken breasts by trimming off any excess fat and unwanted pieces. Mix the spices and cornstarch in a bowl.

Coat the chicken breasts with oil or cooking spray. Sprinkle the spice & cornstarch mixture on the chicken.

Place a piece of parchment or foil in the bottom of your air fryer basket. Place the chicken on top of that.

Air fry the chicken for 16-18 minutes at 350 degrees F, flipping the chicken breasts halfway through. Cook until the internal temperature in the thickest part of the chicken reaches a minimum of 165 degrees F.

Let the chicken rest for 5 minutes before slicing & plating.

Nutrition

Calories: 276kcal | Carbohydrates: 4g | Protein: 48g | Fat: 6g | Saturated Fat: 1g | Cholesterol: 145mg | Sodium: 264mg | Potassium: 871mg | Fiber: 1g | Sugar: 1g | Vitamin C: 3mg | Calcium: 23mg | Iron: 1mg

Garlic Parmesan Chicken Wings In An Air Fryer

Prep Time: 5 min

Cook Time: 20 min

Total Time: 25 min

Ingredients

- 2 pounds chicken wings (or drumsticks)
- 3/4 cup grated Parmesan cheese
- 2 teaspoons minced garlic
- 2 teaspoons fresh parsley (chopped)
- 1 teaspoon salt
- 1 teaspoon pepper

Instructions

Preheat your air fryer to 400 degrees for 3-4 minutes Pat chicken pieces dry with a paper towel.

Mix Parmesan cheese, garlic, parsley, salt, and pepper together in a bowl. Toss chicken pieces in cheese mixture until coated.

Place chicken in the bottom of the air fryer basket and set the timer to 10-12 minutes. After 12 minutes, use tongs to flip the chicken.

Fry again for 12 minutes.

Remove chicken from the basket with tongs and sprinkle with more Parmesan cheese and parsley. Serve with your favorite dipping sauce. We like ranch and buffalo.

Nutrient Value

Calories: 460| Total Fat: 20g| Saturated Fat: 6g| Cholesterol: 94mg| Sodium: 840mg| Carbohydrates: 47g| Dietary Fiber:1g| Sugar: 22g| Protein: 23g|

Air Fryer Marinated Chicken Breasts (No Breading)

Total Time: 5 Hours

Ingredients

- Chicken marinade
- ¼ cup olive oil
- ¼ cup freshly squeezed lemon juice
- 3 tbsp worcestershire sauce
- 3 medium cloves garlic minced
- ½ tsp salt
- ½ tsp black pepper
- 2 tbsp fresh oregano minced or 2 teaspoons dried oregano
- ¼ cup fresh parsley minced and lightly packed or 4 teaspoons dried parsley
- ¼ cup fresh basil minced and lightly packed or 4 teaspoons dried basil Chicken
- 4 8 oz boneless, skinless chicken breasts
- Olive oil cooking spray

Instructions

In a large bowl, whisk together ingredients for the marinade. Add chicken breast to a large container or resealable bag, pour marinade over chicken, seal, or cover.

Chill in the refrigerator for up to 4 hours.

Remove from the refrigerator and let your chicken reach room temperature. (20-30 minutes) Preheat your air fryer to 370° F for 5 minutes.

Remove the air fryer basket and place chicken breasts inside, leaving room between the breasts, so they cook evenly.

Spray each chicken breast with olive oil.

Place back into the preheated air fryer and cook for 10 minutes

Remove the basket and flip breasts over, spray again with olive oil and cook for another 6-8 minutes; chicken is done when the internal temperature reaches 160° F when checked with an instant-read thermometer.

Remove your chicken from the air fryer basket and allow it to rest for 5 minutes before serving! Garnish chicken with fresh oregano, parsley, and/or basil.

Nutrition

Calories:274kcal | Carbohydrates: 5g | Protein: 25g | Fat: 17g | Saturated Fat: 3g | Cholesterol: 72mg | Sodium: 550mg | Potassium: 597mg | Fiber: 1g | Sugar: 2g | Vitamin C: 15mg | Calcium: 71mg | Iron: 2mg

Amazing Buttermilk Air Fried Chicken

Prep Time:15 mins

Cook Time: 20 mins

Total Time:35 mins

Ingredient

- 1 cup buttermilk
- ½ teaspoon hot sauce
- ⅓ cup tapioca flour
- ½ teaspoon garlic salt
- ⅛ teaspoon ground black pepper
- 1 egg
- ½ cup all-purpose flour
- 2 teaspoons salt
- 1 ½ teaspoons brown sugar
- 1 teaspoon garlic powder
- ½ teaspoon paprika
- ½ teaspoon onion powder
- ¼ teaspoon oregano
- ¼ teaspoon black pepper
- 1 pound skinless, boneless chicken thighs

Instructions

Combine buttermilk and hot sauce in a shallow dish; mix to combine.

Combine tapioca flour, garlic salt, and 1/8 teaspoon black pepper in a resealable plastic bag and shake to combine.

Beat egg in a shallow bowl.

Mix flour, salt, brown sugar, garlic powder, paprika, onion powder, oregano, and 1/4 teaspoon black pepper in a gallon-sized resealable bag and shake to combine.

Dip chicken thighs into the prepared ingredients in the following order: buttermilk mixture, tapioca mixture, egg, and flour mixture, shaking off excess after each dipping.

Preheat an air fryer to 380 degrees F (190 degrees C). Line the air fryer basket with parchment paper. Place coated chicken thighs in batches into the air fryer basket and fry for 10 minutes. Turn chicken thighs and fry until chicken is no longer pink in the center and the juices run clear for an additional 10 minutes.

Nutrition Facts

Calories: 335| Protein: 24.3g| Carbohydrates: 27.4g| Fat: 13.6g| Cholesterol 113.8mg| Sodium: 1549.8mg.

Crumbed Chicken Tenderloins (Air Fried)

Prep Time: 15 mins

Cook Time: 12 mins

Total Time: 27 mins

Ingredient

- 1 egg
- ½ cup dry bread crumbs
- 2 tablespoons vegetable oil
- 8 chicken tenderloins

Instructions

Preheat an air fryer to 350 degrees F (175 degrees C). Whisk egg in a small bowl.

Mix bread crumbs and oil in a second bowl until the mixture becomes loose and crumbly.

Dip each chicken tenderloin into the bowl of an egg; shake off any residual egg. Dip chicken into the crumb mixture, making sure it is evenly and fully covered. Lay chicken tenderloins into the basket of the air fryer. Cook until no longer pink in the center, about 12 minutes. An instant-read thermometer inserted into the center should read at least 165 degrees F (74 degrees C).

Nutrition Facts

Calories: 253| protein: 26.2g| carbohydrates: 9.8g| fat: 11.4g| cholesterol: 109mg| sodium: 170.7mg.

Air Fryer Blackened Chicken Breast

Prep Time: 10 mins

Cook Time: 20 mins

Additional Time: 10 mins

Total Time: 40 mins

Ingredient

- 2 teaspoons paprika
- 1 teaspoon ground thyme
- 1 teaspoon cumin
- ½ teaspoon cayenne pepper
- ½ teaspoon onion powder
- ½ teaspoon black pepper
- ¼ teaspoon salt
- 2 teaspoons vegetable oil
- 2 (12 ounces) skinless, boneless chicken breast halves

Instructions

Combine paprika, thyme, cumin, cayenne pepper, onion powder, black pepper, and salt in a bowl. Transfer spice mixture to a flat plate.

Rub oil over each chicken breast until fully coated. Roll each piece of chicken in a blackening spice mixture, making sure to press down so spice sticks on all sides. Let sit for 5 minutes while you preheat the air fryer.

Preheat an air fryer to 360 degrees F (175 degrees C) for 5 minutes.

Place chicken in the basket of the air fryer and cook for 10 minutes. Flip and cook for an additional 10 minutes. Transfer chicken to a plate and let rest for 5 minutes before serving.

Nutrition Facts

Calories: 432| Protein: 79.4g| Carbohydrates: 3.2g| Fat: 9.5g; Cholesterol: 197.7mg| Sodium: 515.8mg.

Air Fryer BBQ Cheddar-Stuffed Chicken Breasts

Prep Time:10 mins

Cook Time: 25 mins

Total Time: 35 mins

Ingredients

- 3 strips bacon, divided
- 2 ounces cheddar cheese, cubed, divided
- ¼ cup barbeque sauce, divided
- 2 (4 ounces) skinless, boneless chicken breasts
- Salt and ground black pepper to taste

Instructions

Preheat an air fryer to 380 degrees F (190 degrees C). Cook 1 strip of bacon in the air fryer for 2 minutes. Remove from air fryer and cut into small pieces. Line the air fryer basket with parchment paper and increase the temperature to 400 degrees F (200 degrees C).

Combine cooked bacon, Cheddar cheese, and 1 tablespoon barbeque sauce in a bowl.

Use a long, sharp knife to make a horizontal 1-inch cut at the top of each chicken breast, creating a small internal pouch. Stuff each breast equally with the bacon-cheese mixture. Wrap remaining strips of bacon around each chicken breast. Coat chicken breast with remaining barbecue sauce and place into the prepared air fryer basket.

Cook for 10 minutes in the air fryer, turn and continue cooking until chicken is no longer pink in the center and the juices run clear about 10 more minutes. An instant-read thermometer inserted into the center should read at least 165 degrees F (74 degrees C).

Nutrition Facts

Calories: 379| Protein: 37.7g| Carbohydrates: 12.3g| Fat: 18.9g| Cholesterol: 114.3mg| Sodium: 986.7mg.

Air-Fried Buffalo Chicken

Prep Time: 20 mins

Cook Time: 16 mins

Total Time: 36 mins

Ingredients

- ½ cup plain fat-free Greek yogurt
- ¼ cup egg substitute
- 1 tablespoon hot sauce (such as Frank's®)
- 1 teaspoon hot sauce (such as Frank's®)
- 1 cup panko bread crumbs
- 1 tablespoon sweet paprika
- 1 tablespoon garlic pepper seasoning
- 1 tablespoon cayenne pepper
- 1 pound skinless, boneless chicken breasts, cut into 1-inch strips

Instructions

Whisk Greek yogurt, egg substitute, and 1 tablespoon plus 1 teaspoon hot sauce in a bowl. Mix panko bread crumbs, paprika, garlic pepper, and cayenne pepper in a separate bowl. Dip chicken strips into yogurt mixture; coat with panko bread crumb mixture.

Arrange coated chicken strips in a single layer in an air fryer. Cook until evenly browned, about 8 minutes per side.

Nutrition Facts

Calories: 234| Protein: 31.2g| Carbohydrates: 22.1g| Fat: 4.6g| Cholesterol: 64.8mg| Sodium: 696.2mg.

Crispy Ranch Air Fryer Nuggets

Prep Time: 15 mins

Cook Time: 10 mins

Additional Time: 15 mins

Total Time: 40 mins

Ingredients

- 1 pound chicken tenders, cut into 1.5 to 2-inch pieces
- 1 (1 ounce) package dry ranch salad dressing mix
- 2 tablespoons flour
- 1 egg, lightly beaten
- 1 cup panko bread crumbs
- 1 serving olive oil cooking spray

Instructions

Place chicken in a bowl, sprinkle with ranch seasoning and toss to combine. Let sit for 5-10 minutes. Place flour in a resealable bag. Place egg in a small bowl and panko bread crumbs on a plate. Preheat air fryer to 390 degrees F (200 degrees C).

Place chicken into the bag and toss to coat. Lightly dip chicken into the egg mixture, letting excess drip off. Roll chicken pieces in panko, pressing crumbs into the chicken.

Spray basket of the air fryer with oil and place chicken pieces inside, making sure not to overlap. You may have to do two batches, depending on the size of your air fryer. Lightly mist chicken with cooking spray.

Cook for 4 minutes. Turn chicken pieces and cook until chicken is no longer pink on the inside, about 4 more minutes. Serve immediately.

Nutrition Facts

Calories: 244| Protein: 31g| Carbohydrates: 25.3g| Fat: 3.6g| Cholesterol: 112.3mg| Sodium: 713.4mg.

Hilton DoubleTree Hotel Chocolate Chip Cookies

Prep Time: 10 mins

Cook Time: 1 hr

Ingredients

- 1/2 cup butter softened
- 1/3 cup granulated sugar
- 1/4 cup packed brown sugar
- 1 egg
- 1/2 teaspoons vanilla extract
- 1/8 teaspoon lemon juice
- 1 cup and 2 tablespoons all-purpose flour
- 1/4 cup rolled oats
- 1/2 teaspoon baking soda
- 1/2 teaspoon salt
- Pinch cinnamon
- 1 1/4 cup semi-sweet chocolate chips
- 1 cup chopped walnuts

Instructions

Cream butter, sugar, and brown sugar in the bowl of a stand mixer on medium speed for about 2 minutes.

Add eggs, vanilla, and lemon juice, blending with mixer on low speed for 30 seconds, then medium speed for about 2 minutes, or until light and fluffy, scraping down bowl.

With the mixer on low speed, add flour, oats, baking soda, salt, and cinnamon, blending for about 45 seconds. Don't overmix.

Remove bowl from mixer and stir in chocolate chips and walnuts. Line the fryer basket with a grill mat or a sheet of parchment paper.

Scoop about one tablespoon of dough onto a baking sheet lined with parchment paper about 2 inches apart.

Air fry at 260F (130C) for 18-20 minutes.

Remove from the air fryer and cool on a wired rack for about 1/2 hour.

Nutrition

Calories:397kcal| Carbohydrates: 30g | Protein: 5g | Fat: 29g | Saturated Fat: 15g | Cholesterol: 55mg | Sodium: 154mg | Potassium: 182mg | Fiber: 3g | Sugar: 17g | Vitamin C: 1mg | Calcium: 34mg | Iron: 2mg

Hotteok Korean Sweet Pancakes

Prep Time: 2 hrs 30 mins

Cook Time: 10 mins

Ingredients For The Dough:

- 1 1/4 cup all-purpose flour
- 1/2 tsp salt
- 1 tsp white sugar
- 1 tsp instant dry yeast
- 1/2 cup lukewarm milk

Ingredients for the filling:

- 1/4 cup brown sugar
- 1/4 tsp cinnamon powder
- 1/4 cup chopped walnuts
-

Instructions

In a mixing bowl, mix all the dough ingredients with a spatula.

Lightly cover the bowl with saran wrap and let the dough rise for about 1-2 hours or until the dough doubles in size.

Punch the dough down several times to release the air in the dough. Then, cover with saran wrap again and let it rest for about 20 minutes.

In the meantime, mix all the filling ingredients in a bowl and set aside.

Line the fryer basket with a grill mat or a sheet of lightly greased aluminum foil.

Rub some cooking oil in your hands and take the dough out from the bowl. Roll the dough into a cylinder shape on the counter surface then cut it into six equal pieces. Roll each piece into a ball.

Take one ball of dough and flatten it between the palms of your hand. Scoop about 1 tablespoon of filling and wrap it inside the dough. Place the dough inside the fryer basket, leaving about 2 inches between the balls. Repeat until done.

Press the balls down with the palm of your hand. Spritz some oil on top and air fry at 300F (150C) for 8-10 minutes, flip once in the middle until the surface is golden brown.

Nutrition

Calories: 137kcal | Carbohydrates: 24g | Protein: 4g | Fat: 3g | Saturated Fat: 1g | Cholesterol: 2mg | Sodium: 155mg | Potassium: 81mg | Fiber: 1g | Sugar: 8g | Calcium: 29mg | Iron: 1mg

Cinnamon Pear Slices

Prep Time: 5 mins

Cook Time: 15 mins

Ingredients

- 1 medium-sized Asian pear peeled and cored
- 2 tbsp butter melted
- 1 tbsp brown sugar
- 1/2 tsp cinnamon
- Granola for garnish optional

Instructions

Thinly cut the pear into 1/4 inch thick wedges.

In a mixing bowl, combine and toss all the ingredients.

Lightly grease a shallow baking pan. Place the pear wedges in the pan, pour whatever is left in the bowl over the pear, and air fry at 340F (170C) for 14-16 minutes until tender.

Pair them with ice cream or sprinkle some granola over them to serve.

Nutrition

Calories: 175kcal | Carbohydrates: 20g | Protein: 1g | Fat: 11g | Saturated Fat: 7g | Cholesterol: 30mg | Sodium: 4mg | Potassium: 103mg | Fiber: 3g | Sugar: 15g | Vitamin C: 4mg | Calcium: 8mg | Iron: 1mg

Rice Cake Spring Rolls

Prep Time: 10 mins

Cook Time: 10 mins

Ingredients

Spring roll wrapper

Chinese sweet rice cake

A small bowl of water

Melted butter

Instructions

Cut the rice cake into rectangles, about 1/4 inch thick.

Cut the spring roll wrappers to the appropriate size, enough to wrap around the rice cake.

Wrap the rice cake with spring roll paper. Smear a little water at the end of the wrapper so the wrapper will stick onto itself.

Line the fryer basket with a grill mat or a sheet of lightly greased aluminum foil.

Place the wrapped rice cake inside the fryer basket. Brush melted butter onto the wraps and air fry at 400F (2000C) for about 4-5 minutes.

Flip the rolls over and brush them with butter again. Air fry again at 400F (200C) for another 4-5 minutes until the surface looks crispy and golden brown.

Let cool about 5 minutes before serving.

Candied Kumquats

Prep Time: 5 mins

Cook Time: 10 mins

Ingredients

- 2 cup kumquat
- 2 tbsp melted unsalted butter
- 1/4 cup brown sugar or to taste depending on the sweetness

Instructions

Cut kumquats in half and pick out all the visible seeds. (Kumquat seeds are edible, therefore it is okay if the seeds cannot be removed completely.)

In a large mixing bowl, gently stir and mix all the ingredients. Then, transfer the kumquats to a lightly greased bakeware.

Air fry at 300F (150C) for 10-12 minutes, stirring a couple of times in the middle until there is a slightly thickened sauce.

Nutrition

Calories: 143kcal | Carbohydrates: 22g | Protein: 1g | Fat: 6g | Saturated Fat: 4g | Cholesterol: 15mg | Sodium: 10mg | Potassium: 123mg | Fiber: 4g | Sugar: 19g | Vitamin C: 25mg | Calcium: 46mg | Iron: 1mg

Pastry Wrapped Rice Cakes

Prep Time: 10 mins

Cook Time: 10 mins

Ingredients

- Chinese rice cake (nian-ago)
- Pie crust or puff pastry
- Egg wash

Instructions

Line the fryer basket with lightly greased aluminum foil.

Cut rice cake into 1/2 inch thick pieces. Wrap the rice cake with pie crust or puff pastry. Lightly press down on the overlapping pie crust to prevent it from opening up. Then, place them in the fryer basket. Brush the top side with egg wash. Air fry at 350F (175C) for 4 minutes.

Flip the rice cake over and brush with egg wash. Air fry again at 350F (175C) for another 4-5 minutes until the surface is golden brown.

The rice cake hardens when they are cold, so it is best to serve them warm.

Nutrient Value

Calories: 384kcal | Carbohydrates: 58g | Protein: 16g | Fat: 12g | Saturated Fat: 2g | Sodium: 44mg | Potassium: 737mg | Fiber: 15g | Sugar: 12g | | Vitamin C: 45mg | Calcium: 127mg | Iron: 6mg

Peanut Butter Cupcake Swirl

Prep Time: 10 mins

Cook Time: 15 mins

Ingredients

- 1/4 cup butter softened
- 1/3 cup creamy peanut butter
- 2 tbsp sugar
- 1 egg
- 3/4 cup milk
- 1/2 tsp vanilla extract
- 3/4 cup cake flour
- 1 tsp baking soda
- 1/2 tsp baking powder
- 1/2 tsp salt
- 1/4 cup Nutella divided warmed

Instructions

Line the muffin tins with cupcake liners and set them aside.

Cream together the butter, sugar, and peanut butter using a whisk or an electric mixer. Then, add the egg, milk, and vanilla extract. Mix until homogenous. Finally, add the rest of the dry ingredients and mix until well combined.

Scoop the batter into the liners about 2/3 full. Then, use a spoon to drop about 1/2 teaspoon of Nutella into the center of the cupcake. Insert a toothpick into the center of the Nutella and create a swirl by making circles in the batter.

Air fry at 300F (150C) for about 12-14 minutes. Insert a toothpick to test. When the toothpick comes out clean, then the cupcake is cooked through.

Nutrition

Calories: 215kcal | Carbohydrates: 18g | Protein: 5g | Fat: 14g | Saturated Fat: 7g | Cholesterol: 34mg | Sodium: 378mg | Potassium: 168mg | Fiber: 1g | Sugar: 9g | Calcium: 54mg | Iron: 1mg

Chocolate Sponge Cake

Prep Time: 10 mins

Cook Time: 15 mins

Ingredients

- 3 large eggs
- 1 1/2 tbsp melted butter let cool until almost to room temperature
- 2 tbsp milk
- 2 tbsp sugar
- 1/4 tsp vanilla extract
- 1/3 cup cake flour
- 1/2 tsp baking powder
- 1 1/2 tbsp cocoa powder

Instructions

Crack 3 eggs. Put the egg whites in a mixing bowl and egg yolks in a large bowl.

To the egg yolks, add in the cooled butter, milk, sugar, and vanilla extract and mix until well combined. Sieve the cake flour, baking powder, and cocoa powder and whisk to combine the wet and dry ingredients to form a thick batter.

In the meantime, use the electric mixer (or a whisk) to beat the egg whites until they can form a stiff peak. When done, pour this fluffy egg whites into the batter and gently combine them with a spatula until it is almost homogenous.

Lightly grease the ramekins and put them inside the fryer basket. Preheat the air fryer at 400F (200C) for about 2 minutes.

Scoop the batter into the preheated ramekins and air fry at 280F (140C) for about 10-12 minutes, until the toothpick comes out clean.

Nutrition

Calories: 156kcal | Carbohydrates: 16g | Protein: 6g | Fat: 8g | Saturated Fat: 4g | Cholesterol: 135mg | Sodium: 89mg | Potassium: 145mg | Fiber: 1g | Sugar: 7g | Vitamin A: 309IU | Calcium: 49mg | Iron: 1mg

Red Bean Wheel Pie

Prep Time: 10 mins

Cook Time: 10 mins

Ingredients

- 2 tbsp melted butter
- 2 eggs
- 2 tbsp sugar
- 1 tbsp honey
- 1/4 tsp vanilla extract
- 1/4 cup milk
- 1 cupcake flour
- 3/4 tsp baking powder
- 6 tbsp mashed sweetened red bean canned or homemade filling to taste

Instructions

Lightly grease 4 ramekins with butter and place them in the fryer basket. Preheat at 400F (200C) for 2 minutes.

In a large bowl, use a whisk to mix the egg, sugar, vanilla extract, and honey. Add in milk and whisk until the mixture is homogeneous. Finally, add in the sifted cake flour and baking powder. Continue to mix until everything is well blended.

The total weight of the batter is about 280g. Spoon about 30g into the ramekin. Air fry at 300F (150C) for about 3 minutes.

Take the desired amount of red bean (about 1 1/2 Tablespoon for mine) and roll it into a ball using the palms of your hand. Flatten it into a circular disc that is smaller than the diameter of the ramekin. Place it in the center of the ramekin on top of the pancake. Scoop about 40g of the batter into the ramekins to cover the red beans.

Air fry again at 300F (150C) for about 3 minutes. Brush some butter on top and air fry again at 300F (150C) for 1-2 minutes until the top is slightly golden brown.

Nutrition

Calories: 284kcal | Carbohydrates: 47g | Protein: 8g | Fat: 9g | Saturated Fat: 5g | Cholesterol: 98mg | Sodium: 101mg | Potassium: 157mg | Fiber: 2g | Sugar: 20g | Calcium: 67mg | Iron: 1mg

Lightning Source UK Ltd.
Milton Keynes UK
UKHW021907290421
382872UK00003B/252